# Naked Bread

# NAKED BREAD

## Bill Holshouser

*for Frank, poetry fan
and helper at Chautauqua,
with much respect.
Bill Holshouser
August 2002*

Every Other Thursday Press
P. O. Box 381888
Cambridge, MA 02238-1888

Copyright © 2001 by Bill Holshouser

ISBN 0-9619960-5-6

My thanks to the editors of the publications in which some of these poems have appeared previously: Ad Hoc Monadnock, City River of Voices, Christian Century, Dark Horse, and Shenandoah.

The members of Every Other Thursday have laid hands, not always gently, on many of these poems, and the poems are better for it. I thank them— Bonnie Bishop, Polly Brown, Susan Donnelly, John Hildebidle, John Hodgen, Priscilla Johnson, Adelle Leiblein, Deborah Melone, Nora Mitchell, Valerie Nash, Con Squires, Phyllis Tourse, and newest members David McCann and Sarah Bennett—for their exacting and competent criticism, friendship, and encouragement over many years.

Three decades of my adult life have been lived among the men, women, and children of the Common Place housing co-op, and more challenging, more supportive, more loving companionship is impossible to imagine. Thank you.

Love and gratitude especially to my family: Jean Chandler, Will Holshouser, Molly Holshouser, Willis Chandler, Kathryn Belden, and Elana Climo

Book and cover design by Anton Marc

Cover photograph of VonCanon farmhouse near Banner Elk, NC, by W. L. Holshouser, Sr.

Back cover photograph by Jean Chandler.

Internal photographs by Bill Holshouser, except 1876 lithograph of William, Mary, and Blanche VonCanon on p. 37, photographer unknown.

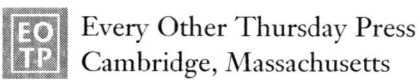

Every Other Thursday Press
Cambridge, Massachusetts

*For my parents, Bill and Louise Holshouser
and for Jean*

# Table of Contents

PREFACE
Jack in the Forest   2

**1.**

Finding Your Voice   6
Skinnydipping   7
Bog Pond   9
Cross Country   10
Roan Mountain   12
The Kingfisher   13
July Hurricane   14
Bill Williams the Trapper   16
Summer Cold   17
Silhouette: Black and Silver   18
And Then There Are Rivers   19
Driving the Damascus Road   20

**2.**

The Elk River Valley   24
Family Album, North Carolina   25
Silence   27
Yellow   29
Grandmother's Garden   30
Things Attics Cannot Hold   32
Sawmill Gravy   35
The Pie Safe   36
Toe River Kill   38
Farming   40
To My Twin Brother Who Died at Birth   44
Jazz in Early Spring   45

**3.**

Why I Live in Cambridge   48

Now They're All Silver   49

Bamboo Fence in Snow   50

Blizzard in Town   51

Turning Point   54

Melting Snow   55

Letter to Andrea   56

Spider Plant   58

Lanterns   59

The Coast   60

A crowd as by a bugle wakened   61

Clear Air Turbulence   62

**4.**

Planning   64

Dubrovnik, 1990   65

The Bridge at Mostar   66

Naked Bread   68

Fledgling   69

Point Reyes, California   71

The Cenote   72

The Wreck of the Laura S. Barnes   74

Montserrat   76

For Walt Kelly   78

**5.**

Job and the Crocodile   80

Carabasset Valley   84

Onset   85

Update   87

The Snake   88

The Cancer Veterans   89

Other Rooms   90

Undressing God   91

The Last of September   93

Schubert: The Posthumous Sonatas   94

Fireweed's Progress   96

St. Francis Crosses to Jerusalem   97

Postscript

The Game of Shapes   101

*About the Author*   102

*Books from Every Other Thursday Press*   103

# Preface

# ❈ JACK IN THE FOREST

### 1. At the Threshold

That was the gate, where the fallen beech
crossed the trail and its stump held up
almost an arm. I grip my stick
and watch for signs. I have passed
into story once more: anything may begin it—
the stone that may be a man
kneeling in a clearing;
                  shapings where sunbeams haze;
three mushrooms with yellow warts.

I had forgotten how rich the air is here,
how one is only not dead
within the frame of a story.

### 2. Jack and his Brothers

These mounds were trees once
but two are my brothers' graves, for I
am always third. One must fail through greed
and be buried on the right. The other, led
by pride, refuses help, and is buried
on the left. Only then does the path
become visible.

### 3. Jack Reviews the Rules

Find possibility: killing flies
may be as useful as killing dragons.

trust bearded men and beggars,
wells and the forest.
                  Believe
that you'll think of something
or overhear the right advice.

Come night, accept the lodgings
you're offered. Share your food
when asked.
          At a crossroad,
throw your hat into the air.
It will find you the right path.

Save white stones, straws, shoes
without mates. Notice everything.

## 4. THE STORY BEGINS

Baying and drooling, someone's hounds
pursue a huge boar across my path.
As unsubtly as that my story
has begun. I do not know what turnings
wait in the teller's mind.
Enough for now that the breeze
in the forest of story
is light on the back of my neck
as the lips of any princess.

I.

## FINDING YOUR VOICE
### —for Erika Mumford

The forest is suspended in afternoon,
pine needles quiet the path. I wander
deeper through the sun's fingers slanting.

A spruce has fallen, or half-fallen,
trunk now a velvet of ochre woodruin
and emerald mosses, a ladder leaning upward
from forest floor to forest roof,
where the sun is climbing.

After a half-hour or more, gradually,
there is a voice here—the tree's, maybe,
or yours—like you, optimistic,
like you, impatient of cowardice:

                            talk
of growth and decay, ferns nurture
their spore, leaves lightly sign the breeze,
pain takes visible form, and some of it
is healed.

          Poets, too, leave
the world's cathedral of predators behind,
yet continue to speak, though it be
as slowly and secretly as trees.

                       I wonder
how long does a voice wait in a clearing?

## SKINNYDIPPING

We were camping together, six families
among ripe cornfields, in good marriages
and bad ones, under a filling moon
and high New England August.

Children asleep, the adults were swimming
in a pond still steaming back the day's warmth,
sheltered from time by the massed song of frogs
from personality by a huge lacework of stars.

After the usual heightened casualness
undressing half turned away, looking
and not looking, there was much to be noticed
much that was different at night:

tidal lift of the moon on scrotum or breast
touch of a foot under water, shadows
between legs dark as woods over the pond.
We moonbathed on a light-soaked wooden float,

chickenfights broke out in the shallows
under flights of a luminous Frisbee.
Currents below the surface laid cool hands
on our bodies, fingering each of us singly.

Then I swam away into quiet darkness
in midpond, ruddered myself into alignment
with the Swan overhead, like Leda at camp,
and floated there, hands open to the night.

There were currents below the stars, too.
There were nerves leading to each swimmer in the mist
each hermit huddled in towels on the shore
and I gathered them all into my hands.

That's how we were bound together—
by nakedness, by revelation, games
and the reflections of games, in silence
enough to see each other's beauty,

a new constellation was imprinted
by the old one overhead, and we were its lights.
Years later now, much is changed—
those same cords stretch into a far wider night,

yet I can feel them pulsing in my hands.
The bad marriages have ended, good ones
still pick their way barefoot over the rocks,
and the cold lays private hands on us all.

Yet each of us is a star, too. There are times
I see it shining through your clothes,
other times it only wrinkles up your voice
or shakes the careless hand that holds your cup.

To strip and swim, go naked into day after day,
touch and be touched, be alone
and reach out, to notice all your strange detail,
to remember it's a joy—there's a game!

But we can't endure it, either, having
so many sexual organs: skin, eyes or noses, bare
minds, palpated by every winter and summer,
the memories of swimmers going out into the dark.

I cry sometimes, because nothing
has turned out as I hoped it would, sometimes
because everything has turned out so well.
Often, in my mind, I swim with all of you again.

## BOG POND

After the opaque passage
of the water lilies, the canoe's prow
scrapes into shallows heavy
as with tea leaves. Nothing floats here
and nothing sinks: stumps, grasses,
mud-jellied carcasses of salamanders
quake in a waist-deep suspension.
There are silt-hung bladder trees
a hand high, and under them a leech swims
like a banner waving in a submarine wind.

Why do they draw my mind,
these shrunken forests, until
I long to walk under them
beneath the sun of the bullheads,
the moon of the water lilies?

It is the seduction of repose:
not death, but life suspended,
the thirst to drink as a potion
the fecundating broth the sun brews
in shallow waters, to rest until
the bones of pain dissolve utterly.

I want to wake up some morning
with clear water in my eyes
and the fathering sun searching
for me with warm, bright fingers.

## CROSS-COUNTRY

We ski easily downwind, downriver, then
late in the day, more tired than we know,
turn upwind, back toward the car.

The day is a percussion work
for wind and mountain: branch creaks
on trunk, dry snow rasps suddenly valleywide,

trapezes over the river, is sieved
through the forest and, sky-high,
slides on a booming wind,

gestures over Mount Jefferson
and lashes past us, raising blisters
of crackle under our skis.

Ahead of me on the trail,
you've begun shuffling, not gliding,
using one pole, dragging the other.

The wind wields the sun like a chisel.
The wind is a wool blanket, whipped
repeatedly over our eyes. The sun is its itch.

On level stretches, I close my eyes,
counting the strides until, nervous,
I must open them and orient myself.

On the river, bales of ice
have buckled upward. We see
black water flowing beneath them.

Together, we are alone, each in our own
battered squint, our headache,
our longing to reach the car—

which we find and shelter in and think,
No danger. There was no danger.
And yet, for a while, we were each alone.

## ROAN MOUNTAIN

The rhododendron let dangle corsages from idle fingers,
shy country girls strolling in mountain pastures
in the raiment of bridesmaids of the blessed.

Rhododendron crowd the higher slopes like a nightclub
of the blessed, their cigarette smoke, mist
flumed upward, scented sax on the wind. Smell
the entrances to flowering subway tunnels:
lilac razors, jasmine nails, destinations
rooted under leaf-mold and dampfire stump.

Read the burls, the hard brown characters
woven by the laurel hell (as they call it here).
What might happen in the rhododendron?
Might we gnarl, feet become knots?

Yes, but this will happen eventually
in any case.
          Today, at least, it is we
who are blessed. Come, run the risk
of this beauty. Walk with me
in back-alleys of the fragrant rain.

## THE KINGFISHER

As if I had kicked loose
the wrong stone, the one that kept
night from this place,
as if a black well was uncapped,
darkness suddenly floods
the valley below me, a lake of shadow
and I on its shore.

Rootless skies of light fall
past me into the lake-bed;
in the creek beside me, leaves file
on currents past the bright bead
of day, grow dim as they flow.
All the colors are sinking,
but the night will not be filled.

Then, unforetold in the red drooping
of this late day, the kingfisher glides
from a flowering judastree draped
over the dark gorge, dives in a wet glaze
and rises. The water that drips
from his sides, brought back from night, glows
like rubies, like blood in burning drops.

## JULY HURRICANE

Horizontal rain, like static
on black-and-white television,
waterfalls at the windows.

The wind plays the old house
like a bamboo pipe, slurs among three notes, or four,
both the snake charmer and his snake.

Behind the rain, behind its own shrieking,
the wind has become solid,
jabs the house, feints, jars it again.

Outside, an oak tree becomes a black disk
of earth and dripping root. Nails screech.
A basement door slams, slams, slams.

Morning. Fields of water mirror a stone sky.
Currents flow gracefully above sunken roads,
an invading army dredging riverbeds

into red clay and rock, full of shredded
tobacco, tangled bean-vines, logjams
of broken corn, evergreen limbs torn from pines.

A baby raccoon floats in an eddy,
a dead snake waves its stream of colors,
a copper power line hisses and crackles.

On the beach, harrowings of wrack,
sand bristled by the wire-brush rain,
starfish in thousands, stiffly stacked,

spongy bowls of jellyfish. (Tomorrow
anemones, then fighting conch, as if death
harvested in waves.) The rain stops.

Farmers come out to grieve, children to wonder,
vultures and grandmothers to scavenge the beaches.
In the sky, the offense of an everyday sun.

## ✸ BILL WILLIAMS THE TRAPPER

There was Bill Williams, ear to the ground
resting in a fresh buffalo chip
and he says to Kit Carson, By God
Kit, I think I hear their spoor!

Old Bill used to go hunting shaky
drunk but whenever he wobbled
he knew how to counterbalance it
with just the right double-wobble
so he could shoot a bullet up a bear's ass
and out its mouth and never touch a hair.

Same way with his wife. He married
a Blackfoot woman who beat him some
but who chewed the beaver hides he skinned
and made those clothes the Smithsonian covets.
In return he closed his eyes and reached
out his tongue and ran it through her pelt
elegantly, like a man tasting a fur coat.
Made it all a little more worthwhile.

## SUMMER COLD

Anyone who's ever tried to flush
a Portuguese man o'war down a pay
toilet knows how I feel today:
eyes sweat tears in tubs of flesh,
bowel quivers like a jelly bucking inside
a bowl, a sac crackling on ceramic reefs.
And lord, the breakers, the spindrift sneeze!
Pay my dimes, I can't quite turn the tide.

What a marsh it is! Slip off the fixed land
of health, the green crabs and fry forage
around. Does the meal still move its hands
and legs? This fever is the heat of their urge,
belly and lungs beached and panting on the sand,
body a living ocean of restless surge.

## ✣ SILHOUETTE: BLACK AND SILVER

That one standing by the window is fading
in the sound of the rain. Cut him out and try
him against some other landscape.
                                      Wash in mountains
around his shoulders, clothe him in vapors
by night, let the trees with their windy arms
throw tear-bright knives through his sleeves
to pin him in his frame.

Or place him for keeping in the gray hands
of the moon, while the points that define
his form scatter
                      as spacious and as empty as Libra,
where Mars may hunt through him
like an angel, as he himself once hunted
through shadow-bright nights and forests
and riverbanks in the mountains, when he first
found he was not afraid of the dark,
and before he grew so tired.

                              Take him where
he will not hear this rain talking to itself
outside this window, where his negative will not
always feel these scissors at its edge.

# AND THEN THERE ARE RIVERS

                   and
                   then
                   there
                   are rivers
so          where silt motes suspended
also        swallow the light a foot deep, drawing
creeks     its warmth along reeds to the eel-inscribed,
wash in,   turtle-stirring mud; where in brown soup herons'
join runs  legs, herons' beaks are teaming scissors striding to kill;
and mountain rivers cold as whistles, juggling sky-colored needles, leaf-colored
  needles, sunlight sparkling in their     shallows, glass rivers pouring
    lights over granite displays, bow     over cliffs, thunder into pools,
     flaking canyon fortresses for fish; and there are hidden rivers, of black water
      mumbling through caverns, deciphering by touch, by blind lap and
      listen, stones no hand will ever fumble on, fallen carvings whose
      curls and grooves are slots where white crayfish slide to feed, rivers buried
      until the      as fate lies coiled in the rubble of events, waiting for
      spring of     the time set to surprise; and vast master rivers, the
      secrets       earth-god's flowing muscle, tolerating for a time
      shall         the buoy on their backs, the city at their
      be,           sides; at whose rising voice buoys
                   bell, and cities rock and
                      tremble.

## ❈ DRIVING THE DAMASCUS ROAD

Pounding tires along the interstate
for hours past flayed recap and flat 'possum
through heat that warps the landscape
around my sunglasses, after a high Virginia
lunch stop (the sacramental red-eye gravy)
I come at last to a two-lane,
to the mountains, to evening
and a storm.

Driving up to Damascus, the road bends
with each bend in the Holston River,
which is white, boiling on its rocks
through hardwoods and rhododendron,
wild in the gravity of the mountains,
rising, as rain like a new tributary
sieves from the sky in long shakings
of gust, pause, gust again.

Rain blinds my wipers, wind
palpitates them, leaves and twigs
befall the car like a county full of the dead,
the road fresh and elusive under my wheels.
The road is a river, the river a falls,
and the evening air a creek full of driftwood
and lightning, wild as hell, and it smells
like sweet heaven,

it smells just made. Gray-green lichen
drink the rainwater in as it courses
through gullies in treebark
and the canyons in fenceposts. I crest
out into Damascus as the sun cuts
a sudden swath between the black sky
and the green river, so I can see
what it means.

It means God summers on the second floor
over the dentist's office, living under
an assumed name and avoiding the local
Baptists except for these surprises
when a flood of horizontal sun radiates
from Main Street and out into the forest—
for the sake, it appears, of the gray-green
lichen, who see it and go gold
at the edges.

2.

# THE ELK RIVER VALLEY

Looking down-valley
from a darkened house:
Mica of stars in a black sky,
mountain ridges lower and blacker,
the river audible among wild iris,
mists pungent with balsam.

I am, in this night, soluble,
knowing by almost touch
where, in the hill's groin,
rhododendron work their knotty puzzles
where the huge chestnut trees lie and rot.

Sheep pasture, a moon begins to rise,
an owl hunts, blueberries ripen.
A stone chimney, standing alone,
crumbles. Cane grows succulent,
cabbages wax in their fields.

Above and behind me, miles away,
a spring rises among the roots of a maple.
A dipper hanging there on a bush
puts its metal taste to my lips.
Two snakes coolly entwine there,

each lost in the other.
                    The water,
stirred by their flow, curls away downhill.
Moonlight.
            A creek smoothes white sheets
over beds of granite.
                    I am on the porch
of the house where my father died.

# FAMILY ALBUM: NORTH CAROLINA

A summer day ripens toward evening. A white
crop of mist grows in the river bed.
My daughter and I hear mockingbirds
singing in the yard. Listen! They
have always sung that way.
                               The woodpecker
flies by, red, black, and white,
a tangle of history.

In the near past a little girl
in a white dress plays croquet, there,
it must have been, where the roots
of the apple tree raise their mounds
by the garden: a tricky slope.

> *I posed in my Sunday clothes*
> *and later married and gave birth*
>   *to your mother*
>   *and five others.*
> *I did what they told me to, but*
> *also played the piano.*
>                   *All the slopes*
> *were tricky. You'll learn about it.*

Farther back, the family poses
on a log porch, children grim
in front, a ham-faced uncle
                         beaming
from behind the corner post. Stories
of snakes crawl through the leaves
behind their eyes. The grandmother

is denied her pipe, though
she still wears a bonnet.

> *Our voices are too yellow and curled*
>   *for you to understand,*
>   *though you will have heard*
> *talk. The blond cousin here*
>   *went to jail later*
>   *for passing bad checks*
> *in a land deal. You'd be less*
> *interested in the rest of us.*

My wife brings us drinks.
As the day cools, we all relax
under the woodpecker's prophesy.
Mockingbirds sing as they have always sung
and my daughter takes my picture.

## ❈ SILENCE

A tear dawns in his eye, runs its course
shining over the gullied world
of his face, and drops
below the chin's horizon.

I say, "What's the matter, Daddy Jacob?"
He says nothing.
                      The elbows of his suit
fret over the wide arms of the green
rush chair. One rocker is split and tarred
by the edges of snagged linoleum.

    He doesn't realize you've gone. Of course
    he seldom remembers you were ever here.
    I rarely think of you either, but always
    of your absence: your absence sits at the table,
    but never speaks; your absence walks at night
    to my bedroom door, but does not come in.

I held the spoon for him. He took his soup
as simply as a plant takes in rain. Now,
as I eat, he sits alone, but his mouth
is still chewing. A meal first eaten and shat
sixty years ago? A breast now buried?

    Don't write anymore. I have no interest
    in Memphis. I don't care if you are a waitress
    or a keypuncher this week. I don't care
    about your night courses. Remember how tired
    you grew of my dissertation? Send money
    if you can, but don't write. Your letters
    are wordy, intrusive, here
    where silence is fallen.

This morning I cut a cabbage, the one
that became soup. Its leaves were like a horribly
warped book. I cut out one wedge-shaped chapter
and ate it in the dry field. It was hot but damp,
the closest I've come to reading for months.

Tonight will be cool. Your absence will walk
in the house as the wind blows through it.
His eyes will stare, old and hard,
into the night. Out of the night a single eye,
far older, will stare back. I will sit,
and then sleep. No one will say anything.

## YELLOW

Driving across Carolina for a weekend
that I know will be impacted with indignities
of mortality, with evidence of my parents' frailty,
I pass fruit trees thin with white, winter-haunted
blossom, jonquils' erect buds itching to come yellow,
and roadside grasses, bent brown, leaching deep greens
from an uncertain warmth in the sun-cold afternoon,
O, heavenly for one just flown in from New England.

My mother and I find fabric scraps
in a cardboard box: wool saved to repair
a moth-riddled crazy-quilt my great-grandmother made,
print pieces rustily pinned to paper patterns,
a shirt she started to make for me when I was 13.
She shows me a yard-high jar
filled with bright yellow corn-on-the-cob, canned, she says,
by her mother, who died in the influenza epidemic of 1918.

Driving back to the airport, I worry: about my father,
his labored breathing, his inactivity,
about the itching on my arm and strange aches in my legs,
which might be symptoms of a brown recluse spider bite.
The boxes we threw out were full of spiders. I pass a farm owned,
I decide, by someone who works for the highway department,
the house and several sheds painted the same mustard
yellow as the center lines flashing past my car.
An embezzler, probably. His forsythia is lovely.

## GRANDMOTHER'S GARDEN

In front of the house, a shady porch, wicker
rockers, her dahlias—famous ten miles
or more around—and lawn, ending at
the two-story wall of grandfather's store.

In back, the garden, full of paths that led,
when I was three, to anyplace worth going—
the nose-wrinkling chicken house, the raspberry
vines and, comfortably, back to the house again.

> "Will, bring the children some candy tonight."
> "Those children don't like candy, do they?"
> "I expect they'd rather eat toadfrogs,
> but you bring some candy from the store anyway."

Grandmother's chopping block was the best thing
in the garden—always good for a squeal
and a shiver when a chicken scrambled, bled,
and flopped, suddenly missing its head.

> "Children, I have two bags here, one with rock candy
> and one with toadfrogs. Which one do you want
> to reach into?"
> "Candy!"
> "That's funny. All my other
> grandchildren like toadfrogs better."

My grandfather died next winter.
They told me he came out
to feed the chickens on a bitter night,
got chilled and took pneumonia.

When we visited next summer, I followed
his footsteps through the garden, touching

the wire fence, the rough gray post
he would have seen when he passed,

and back to the house again, as he'd done,
his death waiting. The asparagus
sprinkled dew on my head as it had
in other years, but I thought of ice.

The worst thing in the garden that summer
was the chopping block. I hid and watched
my grandmother's tired face,
her iron hatchet, the severed heads.

## THINGS ATTICS CANNOT HOLD
—for my parents

1.
When I was ten I stood
in front of my father's dresser,
reached up to the drawer where he kept
handkerchiefs, indian head pennies,
paper clips, and found there a small box
with a gold medal in it, thanking
him in the name of The People
for helping build the first atomic bomb.

That postwar fragment of ribbon and gold
glowed like a fireplace of pride for me,
warming the room so I did not feel
the darkness of huge, cold wings
overspread the globe: the shadow
toward whose winter all
our days now take flight,
the shadow of the ending of years.
Now, forty increasingly cold
years later, I am still warmed
not by the medal or the bomb
but by the man who came into the room
behind me, picked me up, and said
"Don't get excited about medals.
Too many people died in the war."

2.
When I was grown, he showed me
half a metal bolt that once
had held a jet engine to a wing.
"The bolt sheared," he said,
"The engine came partly loose,
slammed itself against the wing
until it tore the wing off

at twenty-four thousand feet. Inside,
nearly two hundred people
watched it happen, and then died."

He tracked disaster to its home,
knew that bolts and engines, all
the dump of things that make a plane,
may be mismade, wear out, are stressed
and have to be maintained.
He saw that guess and error might,
that greed would, co-pilot any flight.
He built an administrator's net
of incentives, regulations—an unpoetic list.
Yet I think, if he reads these lines,
he may like those words the best,
words that mean routine flights,
safe arrivals, lives unlost.
When the People fly, they travel
not only from one airport to another
but through years of thought and labor—
my father's work, for which, I regret
to say, they've given him no medal yet.

3.
My mother said, "I don't trust the North,
Washington or anywhere beyond.
It's not the weather: the people are too cold.
You can be sick and no one knows.
Back home, that would never happen."

Faced with a city of victims,
my mother took them in: runaways
who shared my home, lied about drugs,

who left behind their children
when they ran away from her,
whose children we all fed and bathed
until the parents reappeared.
They still visit her, those parents.
Sometimes, remembering, she calls
me or my sister by their names.

4.
I see her conducting the Reverend
Ralph Abernathy through a church
basement filled floor to ceiling
with donated clothing. In her hand,
she has one stray shoe, and she's saying,
"Dr. Abernathy, if you run across
the mate to this shoe, be sure to tell me."
And he says, "Yes, Louise. I will."

5.
They are going, taking with them
the time when I was young. I want
to call them back and search
their purse and pockets, to find
their younger faces, their jokes
and songs, the sayings they had
from their parents, all those things
that attics cannot hold, that I forget.

Mother, father, how poorly I remember
the dust and air of that time! Yet
what I recall, I turn to your praise.
You have loved well,
you were the pillars of your days.

## SAWMILL GRAVY

Sawmill gravy, my uncle said,
was always eaten by men wearing hats
when he was young, not because
the men wore hats indoors
but because they always ate
sawmill gravy outdoors,
or at least under the tin roof
of a jackleg sawmill, open at the sides,
on biscuits on tin pie plates,
and that sort of men always wore hats
when they went out,
                              not like these days
when men, or near men, wear hats,
or near hats, indoors, and still
often go out with no hat on at all:

pound of pork sausage, brown it,
use the fat that cooks off to make gravy,
mix the cooked sausage back in,
eat it on cut-open biscuits. It's good
on grits, too, or cornbread, or
even on lightbread if it's all you've got.

## ❋ THE PIE SAFE

It was a new state, Arkansas, when the pie safe
was built there, and it was the West,
bordered by the Indian Nation and a part
of Mexico called 'Texas.' Secession and war
were well in the future.

He was a settler, settled enough, at least,
that a heavy piece of furniture, awkward to move,
was not a burden but a possession
worth working to build over the winter
after harvest,

to lever up his domestic economy and scotch it,
to try to hold a bride and a cabin in place
on these plains where all eyes looked westward
but the spring rains sucked it all east,
back toward the river.

He had oak for the body and legs,
thick-cut and planed smooth, but the doors
were red pine, rough cut so the round burns
from a backwoods sawmill blade were
branded in the surface,

and the inner shelves were cypress
dried to an olive corrugation: a bastard
conglomerate of woods-at-hand. The iron nails
were hand-forged, square-headed,
widely spaced.

He used nails, too, to peck constellations
of hole-patterns in tin, covered the round openings
in each door to keep out flies. To keep out ants,
each leg, absurdly small, tapered to fit in a jar lid
his wife could fill with molasses.

As he worked, he noted how his world
assumed the shape of the pie safe, the days
square-shouldered, light-footed, each night
a trunk of cypress-shelved darkness,
less vast than at other times.

He thought, "My work, not my name,
will outlive me, will stand solid, useful,
in unguessable days and places, ant-free,
its feet in another man's molasses,
after I'm gone," and the thought pleased him.

## TOE RIVER KILL

In shady places by the river
were iris blue as memories
of first settlers. Stobs under mud
nudged my feet as I forded
to a rockbed. There, with flat rocks
laid up by the river, I hunted weeds:
milkweed, its fleshy crowns lopped
by stones, the white blood seeping;
goldenrod that  died like cowboys
crumpling from balconies.

Then I found the one rock that fit
all the indentations of my hand,
and I turned to the shallows
where the water god poured itself
over its stones by thousands, treasuring
them smooth with the long thumbs
of its currents.           I was eleven.
I waited, the rock adding its balance
and ease to my own, for living prey.

It was a speckled trout that threw
itself from its pool and downstream
and I threw without aiming
or thinking and hit it! hit it rippling
in the liquid lights of the river,
and now, decades later, I sometimes feel
again the perfection of that throw,
see the stone plunging
to take the fish behind the eye.

So memory has hid in the muscles
of my own arm the lure of weaponry,
and so in part I understand the joy
and tensing of commanders
who stand over continents
watching the movements of peoples.
But I am afraid of what follows—
the fish dead in my hands, a white eye
hanging from a socket, like a small
country that made a dart for freedom.

## ✺ FARMING

House a box of late night, full of its great
silence. Grim voices woke me. Papa, my
grandfather, was downstairs. Two-thirty.
He was lacing up his work boots. Uncle
James, from back corners of the coat closet,
brought out the guns my grandfather kept there.

"Dogs in the sheep," Uncle James told me. I
was a summer visitor, barely twelve.
Unthinkable, childish, to be left home
with my mother, sisters, grandma, tonight.
"Get dressed. You can hold a light," my uncle
told me. "Won't do for the boy to get hurt,"

Papa said. "He's old enough," said James. "He
can help." (It was the summer I helped them
herd sheep through the dipping trough, and so loved
how my jeans smelled of sheepshit and collie
I wouldn't let them be washed for a month.)
"He'll have to stay by the car. Or in it."

We piled in the car, two men, a boy, two
shotguns, two rifles, and Ruff the collie,
but Papa ordered the dog out. "Don't want
him to get a taste for sheep-meat. Once they
get a taste, you can't stop them from killing."
The grass in the headlights was soaked with dew.

No one else on the road. At a dark gate
we picked up Uncle Ben and his shotgun.
A late moon low in the sky, visible
then hidden behind ridges as we drove
the three miles to the mountain where the sheep
were pastured. James, not much older than I,

was also excited. "This is a part
of farming you can't learn at State," he said.
"Do you know whose dogs they are?" I asked him.
"Mostly wild dogs. There's been a pack living
up under Split Rock for two years. But there's
pet dogs, too, that'll run with the wild ones

if they can get loose. They'll dig out of pens,
chew through ropes, crawl under barb wire, once they
get the taste, and hear wild dogs on the run."
We left the paved road. I unchained a plank
gate at the foot of a steep, weedy road,
and closed it again when the car was through,

then ran for the back seat. The car started
before my second foot was inside. We
lurched and wallowed up a rutted creekside
track, out of woods, into a wide, bow-shaped
sweep of cleared land, pasture, dimly moonlit,
curled under and around dark rocks and trees

on the ridgetop. We stopped to listen, heard
the bleating of terrified sheep, barking.
We drove off into the pasture itself,
dodging rocks and scrub, topped a rise, and saw
in our headlights a primitive, nightmare
chaos: sheep, bolting, cutting, frantic, dogs

racing after them, too high on killing
to notice us. We could see four sheep down,
one with a rear haunch eaten away. One
staggered on three legs, dragging a German
shepherd whose jaws were clamped on the fourth leg.
The dog shook its head. We saw the leg break.

Uncle Ben jumped out before the car stopped,
raised a shotgun to his shoulder and fired.
In my flashlight's beam the dog's black side changed
to the color of fresh meat, a pink bright
as Pepto Bismol. James sent a spitz bitch
rolling downhill until a bush stopped her.

Papa, behind an outcrop, fired first one
barrel, then the other. The pack began
to scatter, yelping. James grabbed a rifle
and shot at a black and white terrier
tearing down the slope, a mongrel like my
own dog far off at home. He missed.

I held the light. The men stacked the dead dogs,
five of them. Seven sheep were dead and two
others had to be shot. We left them on
the mountain, to be dealt with tomorrow.
Did we eat sheep that dogs had killed? I was
scared to ask. We often ate mutton there.

One thing more happened next morning. Papa
and James knew the terrier, went to see
his owner, to buy the dog, to kill it.
It was a poor family with a son
younger than I. The boy hid the dog, tied
it in a shed. They found him there, using

his own toothbrush to clean wool from the dog's
teeth, washing blood from his muzzle with soap
and a rag. A little money changed hands.
His father untied the dog, gave over
the rope. The boy cursed and cried, threatened dire
revenge, but the dog was taken and shot.

Some years later, a man—another man—
whose dog had been shot, punched my grandfather
in the face, in town. Papa was, by then
in his eighties. The man would not have dared
hit him if he'd been younger. Papa put
his hat back on, walked on without a word.

## TO MY TWIN BROTHER, WHO DIED AT BIRTH

It grieves me that brothers should take
such different ways after knowing
only each other so many close months,

I to the hospitality of our mother's
breast, to family, you left alone
to turn your body into earth.

You have been to me only the shadow
that flickers over our birthday
when our parents close their eyes.

I cut into a hollow in the cake,
a candle cannot be lit—and you
are here. No, you are always here,

or "here" is a house balanced on
your being where you are. I think you
told me once you only ran a bit ahead,

and when I follow, I will find
your footprints waiting to lead me
to the home and family places of the dead.

## JAZZ IN EARLY SPRING

Downtown last night late
to hear Will's trio play,
the jazz a river,
his solos bright tributaries.
Then Jean in bed,
groggy already with sleep,
rallied to kiss me.

One mountain night
when I was sixteen,
a wind woke the town,
after midnight, and somewhere
a clarinet was playing.
Everyone mentioned it
next day—so sweet a wind,
so warm—as if a goddess
upvalley
had unveiled herself
in the darkness
beyond the last lights
and with that gesture
abrogated all morality,
given universal permission.
I lay in my bed wanting
someone to float down to me,
naked and at once.

I am older now, more
armored or more closed
to stabbings and freshets
of spring and sex. Yet
last night was a like wind,

the same goddess, I think,
reminding me that
though my faith
has grown inattentive,
the shrines of my youth
are still open.

3.

## WHY I LIVE IN CAMBRIDGE

They're basically different approaches
he said.

You can either talk something to death
try to convey meaning by sheer force of words
or you can transform it, show it.

Take us, for example, sitting here
across your coffee table from each other.
We might be symbols, something about Apollonian and Dionysian
or something about the head/heart/mind/spirit/body dichotomy.
Multicotomy,
he said.

Or I, in my rust-colored velour shirt,
might be a metaphor for a more sensuous, embracing stance toward life,
while your suit and tie signify something more defensive
an armoring
or a mask
he said.

As I refilled our slivovitz, talk continued
to swarm from him, forcing his mouth hugely open until
upper teeth passing over the top of his head
he swallowed himself and was gone
left brain
right brain
and all.
Hell of a stance
I said.

## ❧ NOW THEY'RE ALL SILVER

Parking for the symphony, my daughter
and I see cold rubbed like ash
into the creases in the parking attendant's
face, cold wrinkling the frowns
we meet on street corners.
There is winter under winter this year,
cold that spring will not melt.

In Symphony Hall a singer walks onstage,
a winter woman, overweight, her eyes
downcast. She fills with music
and becomes a song that fills the hall.
Her song says, "Deep is pain, deeper
than dreaming. Only joy is deeper."

Molly studies the orchestra
through the facets of her pendant
and says, "Now they're all silver."
For a moment, under the babble
of war and poverty on the wind,
we have all become silver.
We all hear the song we are.

## ❈ BAMBOO FENCE IN SNOW

A windless morning crystalizes
and drifts down, white, upon Cambridge.
The city bristles against the overlay.
At every sidewalk's edge,
urban hedge, chain link, painted board
stiffen under the artless touch.
Only one fence, this one, seems at home
with the unpolished rural snow.

Three horizontal rounds braced
by uprights: left leg, right leg.
Here is a fence with stride,
a posture that a biped can recognize.
(The others, two-dimensional, place
one foot after another on a straight line,
as if being drunk-tested.) See how
it trudges past the greenblack holly.

Modest tan capped in simple white,
it is bound together at every junction
with black rope, like the multifaceted
refraction of a robe tied at the waist,
and each rod in its rounded grip
holds a deep memory
of another place, its home,
as it walks through this foreign city.

I remember, as a child, visiting a city
with my grandfather, a country man.
He never walked by choice on concrete
or pavement, but at its side, on the grass—
if the grass was worn away, then on bare soil.
I am from the mountains. I remember
hollows, rivers, files of folded ridges
that people here have never known.

## BLIZZARD IN TOWN

1.

The night of the big snow
people look up
under the soft waterfall
to an oddly bright sky,
are stirred like cocoa
swirling in a cup,
and spin and fall
for the fun of dizziness.

2.

Thirty feet up
the city-skiers
run (in their minds)
ghost-moguls
that wind flows
by every streetlight.

3.

Parked cars vanish like Alka-Seltzers.
The trudgers take the road.
and the butt-skidders,
the snow-in-the-face-mashers
and their victims
the eyeglass polishers,

4.

amid them all,
the old lady carefully
skating her walker
down the middle of the road.

5.

When the snow stops
we turn a party inside-out,
mush into the drifts
in the back yard
to drink champagne
from crystal glasses
and eat chocolate cheesecake
from each others' reddened hands
in the light of oil lamps.

6.

There is no truth
to the neighbors' reports
of cheesecake fights

7.

but as we wash our hands
in the fresh snow, some
think of low-cut dress-fronts
under jackets, and some
of back-cracks
below belts and underpants,
and snow follows thought.

8.

Two days later the city
is a work of collective art,
sidewalks corridored
into battlements, streets
lined with cubicles
where cars are parked
to be buried by plows.

9.
The sand-and-salt men
follow the plows,
sowing potholes
for a spring harvest.

10.
A thaw, a freeze.
We all become toddlers.
A child throws himself
face first in a snowbank,
which is hard as stone.
His nose bleeds.
He stares at his red blood
in the white snow,
and forgets to cry.

## TURNING POINT

Midnight in midwinter: the dead land laid
in a coffin of snow.
                    As I walk into my yard
each step thumps through a drumskin
that drizzle has frozen. And I too,
when I stop, am quickly glazed:
                                coatsleeves,
boots, eyeglasses glisten as for display
in winter's frozen gallery: "Object
Frozen in Midthought. Medium:
Ice on Man. 1979."

                    Under snow I feel the earth's
stones and furnace; deeper still
the antipodal crust of life; beyond it
the sun, at this moment, passes underfoot
on its way to dawn and delicately
as a mother rocks a sleeping baby is tilted
toward spring.

           And I thank God tonight
for those who first marked this moment. For
the moment has become the creator
of this world and king of jailbreakers.
I have met him here, at midnight
in midwinter, real and invisible
as a baby among refugees, and trust, now,
to find in every winter
a point on fire
with the friction of turning.

# MELTING SNOW

The curbside ranges
are dissolving—white peaks
pocked with gray grit,
black metallic scree
on lower slopes—dust and water
freed from their rigid
winter castings. Clear streams
rinse gutters, fill potholes,
spread into lawn pools
for crocuses to wade;
and the hidden wreckage
rises: broken Christmas
trees, bicycles chained
to No Parking signs,
then mangled by plows.

It is right, in spring,
for compound things
to melt: snow after
its season and I after mine,
freeing God knows what
long-buried junk, dance
away as dust and water
wandering into marriages
diverse as roadsides,
to return in three months
as blue-eyed chicory,
as red bee-balm in six.

## LETTER TO ANDREA

As I turned off the light tonight and closed my eyes,
I suddenly saw your face, or half of it (the left half)
and your shoulder. You were wearing a uniform, more circus
than military, green, with gold braid and a high collar.
Your beauty struck me as it did years ago, like a coil of sun-
light that might refract itself anywhere, in my eyes
or off on the horizon, dazzling whatever it lit on.

I remembered your projects—"You should be better with names,"
you said, and introduced yourself to me without warning
as four strangers, or two, or five, all talking fast
about the election and who made the best cheese in the area
and whether spruce needles are flat or round. Then: "Tell me
the name, age, and work of everyone you've been speaking to!"
—and the lovely way you ridiculed me when I forgot.

And your determination that we must make love on horseback,
your patient search for the right horse, the isolated grassland.
I remembered the olive oil, the bouncy handwork,
and what you called "the push for the summit" that you said
must be genital, the horse's bone and muscle walking under us,
your breast tasting like wet light, horse sweat. It was a dance
and a physics lesson brought to simultaneous orgasm.

We fell off, of course, not into grass, but in soft, red dust,
and not before we reached the summit. Nothing broken—
a stone bruise or two I wish I still had for a souvenir—we washed away
the dust for a long time at a small spring with my ruined handkerchief,
while the horse grazed nearby and watched us, I thought, skeptically.
God knows who else saw us. If anyone came by, I like to think
that he or she thought, "Oh, that time of their lives," and smiled.

I heard that one of your children—an adult already—

died recently (I don't know how parents survive that),
that you might run for Congress somewhere in Missouri.
I'm a middle-aged man these days, I make love in bed,
go to a job, remember most people's names, and think of you rarely.
Every bruise reminds me of you. Spruces, too, and mountain meadows,
and turning out the light, the comfortable dark coming on.

## SPIDER PLANT

When a man comes home after midnight
from a slow supper and some wine
his domestic spiders should greet him
with dignity, with silence gray and discreet
as the paper-thin appraisal that projects
from under the eyelid of a sleeping cat.

But what the hell do I find waiting for me?
Shaggy-shouldered greenery hulking in my window
like a movie ape who might do anything,
swinging on a triple vine of macramé
and bristling about the hour.

I don't know why I bother to live alone.
A man whose feet are unsure
of the precise height of the floor
only grows less steady
bearded by raucous plants.

## LANTERNS

Lanterns turned in the wind.
Lights crossed her face like sunrises
over a familiar country.

She turned to me then,
and the small days passing in her eyes
were morning and night to me;

and in that time I lived
in that country many long and pleasant lives
under lanterns turning in the wind.

## THE COAST

1.

In the warm ocean of sleep
we are swimmers separated and held
together in currents' motions.

Over night's rolling and the swell
of dreams, the slap of your presence:
a foot touches, an arm encircles, backs drift
in proximate bumpings.
                          I float up
into the waves of your waking,
circle with you in the light surf,
am cast up on the day like driftwood.

2.

Yet I like to be away and
awake to watch the geography
of your mind and ways:
                          rocks,
clearings, groves,
vegetation returning after storms.

I stand off your coast,
I roll on your beach,
and you are west
                a new world.

## A CROWD AS BY A BUGLE WAKENED

A crowd as by a bugle wakened
jostles for the reign of my role:
as those whose dreams are shaken
by sunrise, taken by surprise,
rise and take their road,
this crowd, by your kiss so thoroughly,
so suddenly roused, now demands
each one command of speech, hand,
right of rule. I, who am I, know we
feel a fool—so many motley
strangers wrestling in one mind,
while you stand waiting, smiling,
not knowing or only slowly guessing
what political farce your friendly gesture
set loose in these parts.

## ✈ CLEAR-AIR TURBULENCE

My father, studying an airplane crash,
first described wind-shear to me,
how the wake of a take-off or landing
can sometimes, without warning, flip
a following plane or rip off a wing.

There are flights that feel, airborne,
mid-sky, like a trip over boulders
or over the falls. Invisible currents,
unseen solids, play with the wheels
and fuselages of our fortunes.

The lift I feel, always,
when you walk into a room
is also invisible and in wave-form,
the latest surge of an atmospheric
gesture older than time.

So the albatross ride the trade winds
around the globe, landing only when dead air
robs them of buoyancy. I have seen
them arrive after years of flight, "home"
where they were born, and, in landing, lift slightly.

4.

## ❧ PLANNING

A new Baedeker for your birthday
plies us with maps and mileage:
Dubrovnik to Korcula, four hours,
four more by Hvar to Split, then eleven
to Rijeka or fifteen across to Venice.

To run a finger down the indentations
of a coastline, touching places
that grow sensitive as they are held in mind
is to sail on planning's erotic border,
as if the body were an Adriatic
smoothed on its fractal scale,
and the tracing of a way together
a way of making love, each island
veiled in skin, the red and blue
roads a web of capillaries.

A plan is a model, miles mapping to years,
confessing stages together and times alone,
the spire seen in the east against morning light,
the near hills darkening as the sun expunges itself
behind mountains in the west.

That explains the light that falls
over these speculations, the shade
of loss seen for the moment from afar.
What was it we wanted?
To live long and happy lives together,
to have children and grandchildren,
to visit Krk.

## ❈ DUBROVNIK, 1990

Heat bounced from the calcimine walls,
the tabby rooftops—a pinball game
the size of a city under the sun's thumb.
The light was one peal of a golden bell
swelling to afternoon, fading to evening
over the round stone fountain
and its many democratic faucets.
All day we heard coolness lapping
far below at the base of the Adriatic wall,
but in the city it hid under a few evergreens,
awnings and umbrellas at outdoor cafes,
in a well at the center of a shaded courtyard.
Now it rose and favored us.
                                      Hair on arms
lifted in a breeze, eyes relaxed, cool wine
appeared, a salad of tomatoes and onions.
The restaurant was a share of an odd-shaped
wide place in a narrow street. The owner's wife
unpinned the family wash, dried on a line
of demarcation between the restaurant
and a neighboring leather-goods stall.
The owner's daughter brought olives, green, black, red.

God bless the owner, the wife, the daughter.
Keep them safe from the brother
struggling through gray stones and prickly
greenery to the top of the hill, lugging a mortar,
looking down on Dubrovnik.

## THE BRIDGE AT MOSTAR

> "The town's...name is derived from
> *mostari*, 'keepers of the bridge.'"
> —Baedeker's Yugoslavia

The old Turkish bridge at Mostar
arched quizzically over the Neretva
like a stone eyebrow, touching,
at one end, a Croatian side,
and a Muslim side at the other.

At each corner, the bridge curved out
to become a wall above the riverbank.
Higher, the wall opened into windows
of the stone houses and towers
that lined the river on each side:

the town was a continuation
of the bridge by other means.
Its shape was repeated in ornamentation
and rooflines, umbrellas guarding
their cups of shade in terrace cafes.

I have a photograph. Lush foliage
softens both stony banks, holds out
late summer figs above the green water.
In the bridge's single eye, two boys
stand on a flat rock, ready to swim.

And who would want it otherwise? Yet
one of those swimmers killed the other.
Their families blew away the bridge,
severed the town, mined the roads,
clogged the Neretva with bodies and rubble

and blinded an eye that long watched
Europe and Asia reaching out to touch.

## NAKED BREAD

    Flaccid in prophylactic
    polystyrene, this bread
    I bought gratifies no one.
    The careful clerk
    places it in the top
    of my bag to minimize
    contusions from tomatoes.

      Better naked bread
        strapped to motor scooters,
          sopping strong flavors
            backfire, traffic jam, gutter talk.

        Better yet
              bread in backpacks
children coming home from school, loaves
whipped out in play-passion
                turned to swords, to Uzis,
  arriving at dinnertime
      bent and tasty from the trenches.

      Best perhaps
the bread that is brought to Tyrolean homes
      high above mountain villages, carried
up paths that twist like the fingers
      of a baker's hand, then riding in baskets
reeved on pulleys up the steepest meadows
      and penetrated by that diamond air,
a second leaven of palatable light.

## FLEDGLING

A baby bird launches itself
from an ivy-covered wall
in a baroque courtyard in Vienna,
flapping wildly at chin level
through a crowd of men and women
who are sipping wine and coffee.

We move our heads, move our cups
out of the bird's path. If I had opened
my mouth it would have flown in.
It stays aloft but cannot gain altitude,
flies desperately until it disappears
into the ivy on the opposite wall.

Then it's off again at the same
confrontational height, elbowing its way
past noses, hairdos, ears, *viertels*
and mochas, touching down
on a man's shoulder, throwing
itself again toward its green haven.

Is it lost? Is it crazy? Has it been waiting
for a crowd to gather? Is it determined
to learn now, today, while the sun shines?
Neither prudent nor aerodynamic,
it takes flight again, then again, by now
attracting a following of grabby children.

This frantic ball of half-grown feathers,
this terrified airborne toddler
has stolen the day. Parents restrain
their children. Some search for a nest,
others offer their hands as stopovers
in case the bird suddenly weakens.

I've seen children like this, human
ones, seized by a vision of grandeur
but only able to flap, not to soar.
In Batman underpants, with towels
pinned on as capes, they shout *ta da!*
Don't laugh: there's glory in their eyes.

And my own enthusiasms may have been,
at times, a bit too close, too sweaty,
perhaps alarming my onlookers
rather than impressing them,
though I've labored on at whatever
altitude I could manage, trailing my ragged dignity behind.

## POINT REYES, CALIFORNIA

Before dawn, sand trudges wet underfoot,
waves stroke the shoreline
with fingers flat and stretched.

Hills of fog drift and tatter.
Within them, cedars undress,
stand in the light rain.
Fog is a teacher.

Beachrose and poppy, parents and lovers,
float and reach out from a vapor called lifetime.
A sound behind, like two running footsteps
on a wooden bridge, then nothing more.

How beautiful a lover can be,
seen through night and mist,
half find and half offering,
the wind of dawn stirring!

Morning, wash our eyes
to see the shape of who we are, to see
whom we love, walking like cedars
within the tattered fog.

# ✠ THE CENOTE

Like a winged snake from the tropic sky, the sun
drapes heavily on our necks and shoulders
until we find shelter under limestone cliffs
where shaded water flows, clear as a lens, salt

as blood, over shallows and caverns of cave-rock.
We swim there, where once the feathered priests
brought their victims to the sacrifice.

Following the fish below us, your guesses
seek out mystery in sediments on the floor: "There,
in that canyon, a child's skeleton! See its head

bent down onto its knees? And there, that could be
a skull, a shoulder, an upper arm. Still here,
where they threw them four centuries ago?"

Surely they've been removed, I think, even here,
after all this time—all the enemies, archeologists,
tourists. Three feet of water is too little between
us and such relics, the water too warm and salt.

A priest says, "We took only the heart as our tribute,
placed it alive in the lap of the god. The scream cut
across the people's dullness like your crucifix.

"All else, we glorified in this stream.
Under clear water, the body meant more than itself.
It was each of our deaths, our teacher,
it was life, that petal in the tempest of days."

A boy says, "My glory was my twelve years,
my three friends, two green *toc* birds near my window,
the wonder of my body so like the carved gods.
I also liked to swim, in other places far from here."

Both voices fall silent as if waiting for me to speak,
to open the cavern of my meaning, to name like blossoms
the things that I love, to float them on this current
into the greatest silence I have ever heard. I

am not able to answer. Instead, I turn to you
and say, "I think I'll stop swimming now," and mean by it
something enormous about the gap you fill in my life.

## ✺ THE WRECK OF THE LAURA S. BARNES

When I first came to Hatteras Island
more than thirty years ago
the Barnes was a trough
of whitened wood and rust
looming over a self-effacing beach
that held it on display, held it down
with sand, bound it with roots of sea oats,
picked its bones summer and winter,
washed it, washed, and paid it no mind.

Children climbed into the broken hull then
and scaled the ribwall, while their mothers
shouted warnings about rusty spikes.
The braver ones dared to jump down
twice their height to the powder-fine sand.
The marks of their feet
and knees and hands, the canyons they dug,
their bucket-cast towers,
the sea smoothed away every night.

Now I go back, and the Barnes is scarcely
to be seen—timbers exposed underfoot
only at lowest tide, a buried hulk
that loners in plastic caps find
again and again with metal detectors
as they search the coast for Spanish gold.
Water, wind and sand have almost
finished with her now, as if thirty years
were no more than a night's work.

And if there were no shipping, no sailors,
no children—what of it? The earth
is the most permissive of mothers.
The sea, the rain and wind will pick up

after us unworried by memory. I've seen
photos of the Barnes when she wrecked,
an impressive and tragic sight,
but the people on Hatteras cleaned her out
and the earth opened slowly and took her in.
"And what of it?" says the ocean.

## ❧ MONTSERRAT

If he came here for clarity, there is none
to be found. The Madonna holds her child
in her left hand, an orb in her right, and all—
mother, child, orb—are black, ebonized by centuries
among the candles. Or she was always black,
found that way in a cave eleven centuries ago.

Or she was carved much earlier by Saint Luke,
carried here by Saint Peter, then hidden in the cave.
Or it was not a statue, but the Virgin herself
that Saint Peter brought, though they
may have brought the icon, too. Later,
Parsifal found the Grail here, in some stories

though not in all. The monastery floor is a mystic
schematic of the universe. He (remember him? he is
looking for clarity) finds a place in it, but feels
too large, like a person standing in a model. Outside,
the stone is the white-under-pink of uncooked pork,
pinnacles stand like racks of phalluses

above abandoned hermits' caves. It would be
like living in a hollowed-out scrotum,
he thinks. Is that why the monks
no longer become hermits? This mountaintop
is too erotic for that, made by the same Catalonian
god who later made Gaudi to reshape the city.

From a path down the mountain, a long flight
of steps rises, overgrown, clearly abandoned.
He climbs them. At the top, a grove of small trees,
like a model of a grove, and in it a small bird,
the red-brown of fired brick, moves
from branch to branch, sings, and does not fly away.

He sees that the bird is the mountain's thought,
and the mountain the idea of the day
in its white-under-blue sky, and the day the center
of his lifetime. Therefore, the bird—its song, its smallness,
its color, its refusal to flee—is what he learned
today in the sky on this mountain, in this life.

## ✠ FOR WALT KELLY

The 'possum in the striped shirt,
your porcupine in the porkpie hat,
we met them sometimes across
the river from Washington,
in the woods where winos slept.

No 'gator, no catfish, no perloo,
just empty Four Roses bottles
we put in the forks of trees,
and stoned till they shattered.
Everything else, we brought with us.

A kid needs help like yours, Kelly,
to tell a loudmouth friend (an Owl,
say) from a hypocritical Mushrat,
especially around Washington
where Mushrats wax with a wanion.

5.

## JOB AND THE CROCODILE

Job became a virtuoso
of suffering. He sat on an ashheap
outside the city gates
and challenged God Himself
to face him in court.
"Explain it to me, if you can!
The dead children, the boils
like anthills in my skin, explain
even the stolen sheep and camels."

Job saw an arabesque
of light and dust
picking its way casually
over the plain,
through the garbage
and broken pots in the dump
until it sat beside him
and a voice from the whirlwind
called him by name.

> "Job, I wish
> you could have seen this place
> when it was new. It was dark
> when the mountains formed. The sea
> collected in all the hollows,
> and the living things
> began to make their ways.
> Everyone in my family
> gathered to look on.
> When the first light
> suddenly broke in the east
> we all shouted for joy!
> I remember the morning stars
> all sang together. What a song that was!"

"Look at me, I'm dying," said Job.
"My skin is covered with sores
and all I can do is scratch them
with shards from this dump.
I had seven sons and three daughters.
Do You know where they are now?"

> "Job, have you ever looked
> really closely at a crocodile?
> Look at his back some time,
> like a row of shields joined so tight
> even air can't pass between them.
> His teeth are surrounded by terror,
> but his eyes are the eyelids of dawn.
> When he sneezes—light flashes out!
> It's like he could kindle wood
> with his breath. Iron is like straw
> to him, bronze is like rotten wood,
> and his underparts are sharp as broken pottery—
> he could scratch your sores for you!
>
> "Don't interrupt, I'm not finished.
> You should watch a crocodile move, too.
> He spreads himself like a threshing sledge
> on the mud where the water's low
> and makes it boil like a pot!
> He leaves a wake like a torch
> thrown through the air, and he's afraid
> of nothing—ah, there's nothing else
> like him on earth! You could never
> make anything like that, Job."

It struck Job that the ways of God
were stranger than he'd thought.

He found humility in the notion,
and God found cause to bestow
a new life on him—further camels,
children, healing from his pain.

Then God left him and traveled
once again as a dust dervish
to a riverbank where He sat down,
this time beside a crocodile.
"God," said the crocodile,
"The fish in this river taste
like cypress knees, and besides
there's not enough of them."

> "Shut up," said God.
> "Do you ever notice the people
> who come here and catch fish with you?"

"The little ones are tasty,"
said the crocodile, "but the big ones
get loud and throw sharp sticks at me
if I eat even one or two.
I laugh at them. They can't hurt me."

> "You should pay more attention.
> They have good hands, better than anything
> on a crocodile. They build boats
> of reeds and get inside.
> You can't eat them then,
> and they'll outswim you, too.
> It's their minds that fascinate me,
> though. There's no end
> to what they think up—heated
> houses, calendars, makeup,

philosophy, alimony. Listen to this!"
God sang a few measures of *Die Forelle*
while the croc salivated
appreciatively. "They'll think of ways
to catch every fish in the river,"
God mused, "and then they'll starve
because the fish are gone.
They're clever, but they don't seem
to think ahead very well."

"They sound like a damn menace," said
the crocodile. "Speaking of fish, now..."
"Shut up," said God. "Look,
do that thing where you make the water
boil like a pot. That always knocks me out."

These conversations are a big part
of God's work. What's the point? you may ask.
Sometime in the future, in heaven,
when Job is resting beside a river,
a crocodile will crawl up
and lie beside him and ask,
"Did you folks ever learn
to work things out with the fish?"
And Job will answer, "At best,
I guess we only muddled through it.
Look, would you show me how
to do that threshing-sledge trick
I've heard so much about
if I teach you to tie a clove hitch?"

## CARABASSET VALLEY

I am lying in the sun
on a rock in mid-river,
white water curling past.

When I was twenty
and had the right shoes (and legs)
I'd race the water down

from boulder to boulder, defying
Heraclitus: I've often stepped
in the same river twice.

Tree-trunks shoot upward,
explode above me
into slow August fireworks.

*Who is it here,*
*who feels April*
*at his back*
*in the rock,*
*midsummer*
*in his face,*
*rushing water*
*on either hand?*

In no time, time passes.

## ✺ ONSET

The afternoon begins to crumble around him.
It constricts over his head to a narrow dome,
bell-shaped, transparent,
on whose surface ice sheets slide downward,
who knows how far? He grows colder.

As a child, he had dreamed he was trapped
in a blizzard in a paperweight, tracing fearful
patterns where his breath steamed the concave glass.
But there had been a snowman, a spruce,
cottages with hopeful, lighted windows.
Here, it only grows darker.

He remembers playing alone, once,
in a strange house on a winter evening.
When the room grew dark, he could not find the lights
and so made himself as small as possible
keeping in the exact center of the room
away from the darker shadows
in corners, under tables, in doorways.
He found four perfectly round marbles in an ashtray
and rolled them across patterns in a faded rug,
played a tiny golf game with a maroon vase for a green,
thin *Werkstaette* tendrils flowing from it
as fairways and bunkers. The ceiling was too high;
a wooden fan turned there like a bird of prey.

There had been no time; it was
disorienting, but also spacious.
Here, he is no longer a child.
and time crowds in so tightly
that breathing becomes difficult. He thinks
the sheets of ice slipping past
are wrinkles in his forehead,

so tightly does he want to shut his eyes.
Outside his constricting world
the giant bird again spreads its wings.

## UPDATE

If I understand what my doctor is telling me,
I have a fatal disease which I'm trying to cure
with a near-fatal treatment which is being interrupted
by a potentially fatal complication which I'm treating
with a (merely) rather hazardous drug.
                                                  I find I'm enjoying
the whistle and nudge of passing ironies,
feeling like an 8-ball in a break
or a very lucky child playing in traffic.

## THE SNAKE

The snake is thin as spaghetti.
The snake is transparent.
He sinks his one fang in my arm
and hangs there for hours
dripping poison in
from bloated sacks.

In the snake's world
there is no time
but there are effects: a bad
bargain. I feel him
crawling like stitches
through my colon.

I want to fight the snake,
but he says "Live through it,
we're on the same side.
Visualize something warlike,
and be sure we win in your mind.
It might make a difference."

The snake is my physician.
I am collaborating
with my poisoner.
There are worse things,
I tell myself, sick of him,
things worse than the snake.

# THE CANCER VETERANS

They are slow to talk about these things, even among themselves.
How the blunt diagnosis lodges in the mind, then, with time,
sinks into the body, how it sticks and freezes in tissue and organs.

How they first woke after surgery, before painkillers the killer pain.
How wounds in the mirror scar eyes that see them.

How they were with grudging consent drafted to be damaged,
who see a large sweet world where they lived once, and may not go in.

How they are kin to these damaged others, the hairless, the sticklike,
those vomiting behind closed doors, those so small
behind helium cheerfulness, the irate and demanding, the diligent students
of non-elective subjects, those new to the fire, those burning out.

This is their parade. They walk in corridors pushing metal poles,
from which dangle their external veins. Colorful fluids drip. They walk
in slippers that will not mate, and call one shoe hope and one despair.
They may not wave to you from the float. Still, cheer them as they pass.

## OTHER ROOMS

There are places not my home—
houses, rooms, even fields—
where I have been living for years
though I don't remember noticing:

a cabin by a rainy river,
a room newly painted white,
a vineyard rusty with autumn grapes,
a third-floor walkup by the trolley line.

And there are people in those houses
just finishing a sentence, waiting
for a question to be answered, watching me
as if I had just spoken to them,

as if I were familiar there. I
have been living with those people, too,
in no static way, arguing with them,
learning, loving them, it seems

though some are dead and others far away.
Why didn't I know?—my daily sights,
sounds, wife, job are one room,
often the largest, in the house I live in,

and there are many rooms, more
as I grow older, and what I know
in one I know in all, like a chord
listening to itself, living in every note.

## UNDRESSING GOD

1.

As the math tells it, we were all together
in our first nanoseconds as a universe
at Planck density: youthful energy!
But since then, entropy.

Maybe we needed space.
Hydrogen evolved. Matter outweighed light.
Stars spun off, and planets.
Rocks congealed in the mineral broth,
thrust upward in tectonic tosses.

Now headstones of continents wear away
like stone lambs over dead children.
How old it is, everything that we see.
How inexorably it ages. Only you who made it
remain as young as ever, fire just kindled,
clear spring in which we are still rising,
where light and matter are one.

2.

Our fathers have draped you
in their sex, fatigue, and whiskers. Adjectives,
reverence, resentment weigh you down.
Our mothers have begun to deck you out
in gowns and pronouns of their own.
You are enthroned as if you could not stand.
Enough! There is blasphemy to be done!

I lift the crown from your head,
heavy staff and orb from your hands.
Now that fake beard and the frown behind it.
Then the robes, even the Sistine loincloth.
Let's see about this gender controversy!

From your eyes, let me wipe away
the sense of having seen it all one time too many.
(Not the tears or the joy, I suspect they belong.)
Now. Give me a moment to hide my eyes.
Run your hands through your long hair,
shake it loose, the way Buonarroti saw it.
Be who you are.

## THE LAST OF SEPTEMBER

...is about endings, surely, the lost summer
reflected in spheres of fox grapes *halbtrocken*
among yellow leaves. Flash stabs of sun
assault at eye level through thinning forests
and the harvest dries down to root cellar,
smoked meats, Mason jars. Daily, daylight dwindles.

People often say, These two hours in a red-and-yellow
valley, this one embrace, this transfiguration of talk,
if it may never happen again, is enough for a lifetime.
Sometimes, though not often, this is true. Walking
calf-deep in rattling leaves, I once tripped
on a sleeping dog, once uncovered a frightened snake,

and was glad of it both times, but the leaves alone,
with their airy drag and rumors underfoot, are also alive.
May we walk again, embrace, and wink back at the hundred
round eyes in the grapevines. . . but if not, may the food
of this harvest carry us through winter, and the wine
of late September bloom in any glass where it's poured.

## SCHUBERT: THE POSTHUMOUS SONATAS
—for Alfred Brendel

Three days out the vacationers
begin to notice details: how fish, leaping,
glitter in the ship's wake,
the push and flutter of varying winds.

> Red bells open in the mountains
> over gesturing sea-green leaves.
> The flower is called the beautiful lady.
> She turns to north, to east
> in the April wind.

A storm gathers at sea.
Passengers leave the sun deck;
their chairs are folded and stored.

> A wanderer falls ill in a remote
> village, after a morning on a sunny
> road. He is given a bed
> in a room off the local
> tavern. The owner and his wife
> bring him turnips
> which he does not eat.

>> Images float on his fever:
>> tea darkly translucent in thin
>> porcelain cups; a singer
>> standing just out of hearing;
>> a red flower
>> that brightened one rest
>> in a mountain meadow; a woman,
>> her eyes too large and bright,
>> who turns her face away.

> He looks at his hand and thinks
> What a waste! Those fingers
> would be good for years yet.

The storm now covers land and sea.
Night falls in the mountains,
the wind from the north. The cells
of the flower are freezing, its
fiber wilting. Red spiders
wait under limp, curling leaves.

> The wanderer is buried. He hears earth
> overhead, stamped by boots.
> His fever is gone.

Storm rains curtain the ship. The captain
orders a concert to calm
the vacationers, but the sea
breaks in: cold spray strikes the audience,
they feel water around their shoes.
The chamber orchestra plays
Beethoven, at first well,
but then with increasing distraction.

> It is not the world
> sinking into darkness.
> It is each thing
> in the world, its songs,
> each object held in mind,
> each view from a road
> each face of love
> disintegrating at the end.

## ❧ FIREWEED'S PROGRESS

Fireweed climbs itself like a ladder toward autumn,
the ruin of the lupine has come again,
and I am shocked to learn once more that my life
is not perennial but anecdotal. Indian pipes appear
among fallen leaves and acorns, the corpse flowers.

Don't get poetic on me. I am not my son.
Any eyes he sees in the forget-me-not are different eyes,
the stories the touch-me-not tells me are mine.
From the ground, I see a tanager and think him beautiful.
What the tanager sees—don't we wish we knew?

## ST. FRANCIS CROSSES TO JERUSALEM

I remember I was born and lived
for a time.  Then we set sail from Venice,
my lady mother and I.  I remember that damned
wind's hair streaming in my face all night
and two fingers of rain in the sky.
Not a bad time for crossing, all in all,
though most below decks were ill.
Then a change for the better at dawn:

small breezes swung on morning's turnbuckle
as we landed at Acre and loosed the animals.
The birds revived quickly and told us of the land ahead
open and fruitful to the horizon. Leopards
ranged widely, bringing us pears and nuts
in baskets. No one knew how far
it might be to the city, but we set out
carrying the smaller snakes and rodents.
The sun was shining and we were all singing.

# Postscript

## ✠ THE GAME OF SHAPES

In a festival of the demigods,
for amusement, Manawydan opened
his leather bag, released a rabbit and
a fox. He took a rope and let it rise
and tighten, slanting up beyond seeing
into the sky. The fox chased the rabbit
up the string, becoming a little boy
as the rabbit changed to a little girl.
They grew older as they ran upward. Then
the man (as he had become) in teasing,
ran unevenly, upset the woman's
balance—a string is a narrow path—
so she rocked, screamed a high thin scream high in
a clear sky, fell and smashed bloodily
among the spectators. Manawydan
called angrily to the man, who became
a fox again, ran down the string into
the bag. The god whispered to the woman.
She hopped, now a rabbit, into the bag
which Manawydan drew closed. Moreover
Manawydan stepped back into his story,
which folded itself into a book.
Look, you could hold it in your hand.

## *About the Author*

BILL HOLSHOUSER was born in Blowing Rock, North Carolina, in 1939, and grew up in and around Washington, DC, where his father was a government scientist specializing in airplane crash investigation and his mother a frequent volunteer for many causes. He worked as a Presbyterian minister and was deeply involved in the civil rights movement in the 1960s in Virginia and Arkansas, when he also worked as an organizer of voters, students, consumers, and interracial dialogue groups. After earning a degree in city planning at Harvard, he worked as a consultant evaluating government and nonprofit housing programs and as director of information technology at the Cambridge, Massachusetts, Housing Authority. He has also lived in Austria and traveled in Europe, North, South and Central America, and Asia. He is a founding and current member of Common Place, a Cambridge housing cooperative begun in 1971. He is married to Jean Chandler, a university professor, and is the father of three adult children. He began writing poetry in the 1970s as a student of Harold Bond, and has been a member of the Every Other Thursday Poets for almost twenty years. His poetry has been published in *Dark Horse, Southern Poetry Review, Shenandoah, Christian Century, City River of Voices, Ad Hod Monadnock*, and other journals and anthologies.

## Books from Every Other Thursday Press

*Witness and Wait:13 Poets from New England*, anthology
*Something Understood*, anthology
*Willow Water*, Erika Mumford
*Words for Myself*, Erika Mumford
*Tenderly Pressed: A Memoir in Poetry*, Susan Donnelly
*The Ether Dome*, Susan Donnelly
*Blue Heron Stone*, Polly Brown

To purchase books, write for information to:
Every Other Thursday Press
P.O. Box 381888
Canbridge, Massachusetts 02238-1888

## Other Books by Poets from Every Other Thursday

*Eve Names the Animals*, Susan Donnelly (Northeastern University Press)
*Greatest Hits*, Susan Donnelly (Pudding House Publications)
*Transit*, Susan Donnelly (Iris Press)
*Defining Absence*, John Hildebidle (Salmon Poetry)
*The Old Chore*, John Hildebidle (Alice James Books)
*One Sleep, One Waking*, John Hildebidle (Wyndham Hall Press)
*In My Father's House*, John Hodgen (Bluestem Press)
*Bread without Sorrow*, John Hodgen (Eastern Washington University Press)
*Keeping Time*, David McCann (Troubadour Press)
*Proofreading the Histories*, Nora Mitchell (Alice James Books)
*Your Skin is A Country*, Nora Mitchell (Alice James Books)
*The Door in the Forest*, Erika Mumford (Green River Press)
*The Karma Bazaar*, Erika Mumford (Taylor's Point Press)
*The Narrows*, Valery Nash (Cleveland State University Press)
*October Swimmer*, Valery Nash (Folly Cove Books)
*Dancing with the Switchman*, Conrad Squires (Pudding House Publications)